A School Leader's Manual for Opening a New School

A School Leader's Manual for Opening a New School

How to Plan and Be Ready for the First Day of School

Jane Garraux

Palmetto Publishing Group
Charleston, SC

A School Leader's Manual for Opening a New School
Copyright © 2019 by Jane Garraux

All rights reserved
This book or any portion thereof may not be reproduced or used in any manner whatsoever without the express written permission of the publisher except for the use of brief quotations in a book review.

First Edition

Printed in the United States

ISBN-13: 978-1-64111-538-4
ISBN-10: 1-64111-538-6
eBook ISBN: 978-1-64111-603-9

TABLE OF CONTENTS

Preface vii
Introduction ix
Funding xi

Chapter 1   Mission/Vision 1
Chapter 2   Furniture, Fixtures, and Equipment 6
Chapter 3   Technology 11
Chapter 4   Athletics 15
Chapter 5   Media Center 19
Chapter 6   Accounting 21
Chapter 7   Policies and Procedures 23
Chapter 8   Handbooks 27
Chapter 9   Safety 35
Chapter 10 Schedules 40
Chapter 11 Instructional Materials 46
Chapter 12 Personnel/Hiring Process and Leadership Positions ... 48
Chapter 13 Business Partnerships 53
Chapter 14 Parental Involvement 56
Chapter 15 Professional Development 58
Chapter 16 Communication 60

Epilogue 63
Acknowledgments 64
References 65

PREFACE

After spending thirty-eight years in public education and being involved in opening three schools, I became keenly aware that there were no detailed resources for the process of getting a school up and running. While each school district is unique procedurally, the overall concepts are consistent. The goal of this manual is to provide information from a school site administrative perspective that can be used as a whole or in part. Even if only one idea or model is helpful, then this book will be an invaluable resource for school districts across the country.

I began my career as a teacher but quickly moved into administration after ten years. The experiences I have had over the years have forged my thinking about what it takes to open a new school, which I have done in three different schools in three different capacities.

I was hired as a teacher in a new high school in the fourth largest school district in the United States. This high school opened with grades nine through eleven and over thirty-five hundred students. While I was not involved initially, I was moved from teaching into an administrative role a few weeks after the school year began. I was charged with working with the existing policies and procedures, and then I began to revise and adapt them to the school community.

My second school opening was as an assistant principal. The newly appointed principal and I were reassigned from our previous schools six months prior to the open date. The school proposal was for an academy-based high school with a projected four-year enrollment of over four thousand students. We were allowed to hire clerical staff and department heads for planning purposes. As the assistant principal for curriculum, I was assigned the responsibility for the development of all of the academic programs as well as policies and procedures.

My last school opening was as a middle school principal in the school district of my hometown. I retired from my previous district but could not pass up the opportunity to open a new, state-of-the-art school in the town where I grew up and attended public schools. I was hired one year prior to the school opening and was responsible for all aspects of the process with the exception of the building design. This school was designated as a Science, Technology, Engineering, Arts and Math (STEAM) school for the district with a projected three-year enrollment of one thousand students. The planning team of five started approximately six months prior to the school opening.

In my extended career, I have no regrets. I have worked hard over the years, and the rewards have been enormous. There is no greater experience than opening a new school, but it takes an unbelievable commitment. There were many long days and late nights that extended for multiple years. One of my most famous sayings is that it literally takes five years to open a new school: one year of preplanning and four years to constantly tweak the policies and procedures.

I am grateful for the thousands of colleagues I have worked with over the years. Each of those connections has become ingrained into my leadership style and helped me as I made school site decisions. Without each of those contributions, I would not have had the necessary skills to open a new school. It is my hope to share some of those experiences in a manner that promotes public education.

INTRODUCTION

Based on my experiences, I have found that the school superintendent, in conjunction with the school board, determines when, where, and what type of school will open. In that process, the general decisions will be made based on the needs of the community. New schools typically open as a relief for a growing population or as a replacement for an existing, older building. In both examples, the superintendent and school board carve out expectations and a basic vision for the educational programs.

Once the superintendent and school board approve the opening of a new school, the process begins. The district planning and/or facilities department secure the architectural designs for the building based on the vision and approved funding. Depending on the timelines for school site administrators to become involved in the process, this manual begins with the expectation that input will be solicited from the initial review of the architectural plans.

Since opening a new school is not a scripted process and varies with each district, the organization of this manual is not specific to the planning process. Chapter One is a starting point, and it is recommended to begin there, but after that, each chapter is predominantly independent in that the reader can begin and end where needs dictate.

FUNDING

Decisions that are made regarding the facilities, technology, athletics, media center, and almost everything beyond the policies and procedures are determined by the funding allocations. Based on my experience, I know school districts have unique methods of funding, and it varies from district to district. The first step must be a meeting with district representatives to discuss the actual dollar amounts and the dollar amounts for each category. For instance, I worked in one district that had a separate allocation for multiple categories: athletics; media center; technology; furniture, fixtures, and assets (FFA); and personnel. Another district completed the FFA, technology, and media center purchases with little or no input from the school leadership. A separate allocation was made for athletics and incidentals.

Whatever the process, the parameters for expenditures must be identified at the onset of the planning and selection process. Additionally, if allocations are provided and there is flexibility for purchases, it is recommended that a substantial dollar amount be held back until the deadlines. Invariably, crucial items are left off lists and/or ongoing assessments determine the need for additional purchases.

Chapter One:
MISSION/VISION

As mentioned, the starting point of opening a school is an academic framework. The school district most likely has determined the theme and, in some cases, even the mission and vision statements of the school. With that in mind, the planning process begins either with what has been provided or the creation of the mission or vision statements. These statements provide a school with an overview of what professionals want to accomplish and how they hope to meet those expectations. The schools that have been the most successful in addressing the overall academic achievement have benefited from a clear and concise purpose that is developed from a shared set of core values as reflected in the vision and mission (Gabriel and Farmer 2009).

The vision statement of a school is defined as a collective expression of the school's goals. The mission statement is an overview of the strategies to achieve those goals. The development of these statements should include as many stakeholders as possible. The inclusion of such stakeholders is dependent on the identification of those groups and the timeline for the student enrollment process. Both the vision and mission statements can be created initially with little input; however, it is imperative that once the stakeholders have been identified, these statements are reviewed and modified as needed (Gabriel and Farmer 2009).

The statements vary from school district to school district and from school to school, depending on the age of the student population. Below are a couple of examples of each from the three grade levels: high school, middle school, and elementary school.

ELEMENTARY SCHOOLS

Alexander Elementary School—Greenville County Schools, SC

- **Vision:** The vision of Alexander Elementary is to produce scholars that are successful and empowered to compete globally based upon their own unique talents and interests.

- **Mission:** The mission of Alexander Elementary is to build a community to Embrace, Engage and Empower, Everyone, Every day!

Wesley Matthews Elementary School—Miami-Dade County Public Schools, FL

- **Vision:** We are committed to provide educational excellence for all.

- **Mission:** Our "Universal School," composed of students, school staff, family members, and business leaders, is committed to the process of educating creative and successful future citizens in an ever evolving, multifaceted community. Each child's unique intellectual and affective needs are addressed through innovative, dynamic, and relevant approaches to teaching and learning.

MIDDLE SCHOOLS

- *Southwood Middle School*—Miami-Dade County Public Schools, FL

- **Vision:** Southwood Middle School endeavors to be a warm, creative learning environment where students will develop the strengths to overcome academic and social challenges.

- **Mission:** Southwood Middle School is committed to preparing today's student to become a productive, responsible, and self-reliant citizen ready to meet the challenges of tomorrow's technological and multicultural society.

Dr. Phinnize J. Fisher Middle School—Greenville County Schools, SC

- **Vision:** The STEAM middle school will provide a continuous pathway of education through opportunities that create STEAM-literate graduates ready to accept the challenges of the curriculum at high school, advanced education, and the needs of tomorrow's workforce. Innovation is the key to discovering the solutions to the challenges facing the world today and in the future.

- **Mission:** STEAM (Science, Technology, Engineering, Arts, Math) Education seeks to transform the typical, teacher-centered classroom by encouraging a transdisciplinary curriculum that is driven by problem-solving, discovery, exploratory learning, and an experience that requires each student to actively engage in a situation in order to find its solution. The STEAM curriculum permeates every facet of the school environment from the moment the student steps onto the campus until he or she advances to high school and the postsecondary world.

SENIOR HIGH SCHOOLS

J. L. Mann High School—Greenville County Schools, SC

- **Vision:** Making a difference by inspiring, supporting, and preparing students for their next steps in life.

- **Mission:** We develop opportunities for all students to achieve personal success and become college and career ready in order to become productive, responsible, and engaged citizens.

Center for International Education—Miami-Dade County Public Schools, FL

- **Vision:** Our vision is to create confident, responsible, reflective, innovative, and engaged learners.

- **Mission**: The Center for International Education is dedicated to working with all stakeholders in providing the highest levels of education to its learners. Our mission is to deliver a world-class education through the provision of high-quality curricula, assessments, and services. We aim to develop learners who are confident, responsible, reflective, innovative, and engaged. Our graduates will position themselves as models of academic excellence in a global community and will be equipped for success in this fast-changing, modern world.

Mast@Homestead Senior High School—Miami-Dade County Public Schools, FL

- **Vision:** The Medical Academy for Science and Technology is dedicated to cultivating the next generation of health care professionals through science, technology, engineering, and mathematics while increasing the commitment to community service.

- **Mission:** MAST@Homestead pledges to provide a medical health science high school academy recognized by its formation of students seeking careers in health care and science research through a challenging curriculum that exposes them to critical thinking, engineering, technology, mathematics, science, field studies, projects, competitions, and scientific research. MAST@

Homestead is committed to forge individuals who will become leaders in the medical field, be dedicated to public service and social responsibility, and facilitate the health care needs of our ever-changing, global community.

The vision and mission of a school create the school culture from the onset. It is essential to have a well-defined purpose that expresses an idea for future success and achievement of all students as you plan. The blueprint must be concise, clear, and outline the necessary strategies that are to be utilized by and for all stakeholders. These strategies are developed through collaboration and achieved as a cohesive group.

Chapter 2

FURNITURE, FIXTURES, AND EQUIPMENT

For the purpose of this manual, the actual building design has been approved by the school board. In most cases, the decisions regarding the interior furniture, fixtures, and technology are to be determined by the principal and/or administrative designees. If this is a new school and not a renovation or new building for an existing school, the starting point for this process is to identify the school colors. It is important for all grade levels but even more essential for secondary schools. The school colors will be tied into the gym colors, athletic uniforms, and, if required, school uniforms. If the stakeholders are not known during the planning process, the administrative designee and/or district representatives will need to temporarily select the school colors and a mascot.

School colors and the mascot should be determined after researching neighboring schools, and they should be unique to your school. School colors and the mascot are instrumental in helping to create school unity and establishing a school culture. It is recommended, if possible, to solicit input from stakeholders; however, those decisions may need to be delayed until a minimum number of stakeholders are identified and available. If the stakeholders are identified at the onset of the planning process, it is recommended that the school colors and mascot be decided in tandem with their input.

Many of the items that are presented in this chapter will be in lists and are self-explanatory. There may be a brief notation, but these lists are dependent on the process of each school district.

Decisions for furniture selections are based on the grade level, enrollment, curriculum, location, and cost. It is strongly recommended that furniture purchases include the projected final growth enrollment. Plan for the long term and growth factors to ensure uniformity and the unpredictability of enrollment factors. Make sure to include flexible configurations to accommodate the school curriculum, especially if it is identified as a themed school (i.e., Science, Technology, Engineering, Math [STEM]; Science, Technology, Engineering, Arts, Math [STEAM]; and International Baccalaureate [IB]).

The following items should be included in the furniture, fixtures, and equipment selections:

- Student desks
- Teacher desks
- Administration desks
- Counselor desks
- Media specialist desk
- Nurse desk
- School Resource Officer (SRO) desk (if applicable)
- Clerical desk
- Cafeteria managers desks
- Plant engineer/head custodian desks
- Planning room desks
- Chairs for all desks
- Tables for both classroom and work areas
- Chairs for student tables/worktables
- Podiums for the classrooms
- Podiums for presentation areas: auditorium, cafeteria, gym
- Table for computer docking station to Promethean/SmartBoards (if applicable)
- Bookcases for classrooms and offices
- Filing cabinets and/or storage cabinets
- Science hazard storage cabinets
- Fireproof file cabinets for student records
- Conference room tables
- Conference room chairs

- Main office lobby furniture
- Seating for individual offices
- Trophy cases

GYM

- Chairs (if used as an auditorium)
- Chair racks
- Large projection screen (if used as an auditorium)
- Projection equipment (if used as an auditorium)
- Sound system
- Floor cover to avoid damage from the chairs
- Shelving for physical education equipment
- Shelving for athletic equipment storage
- Washer/dryer
- Physical education locks

HEALTH ROOM

- Beds
- Refrigerator
- Washer/dryer

SCIENCE ROOMS

- Lab tables
- Chairs
- Hazard/chemical storage
- Refrigerator

MUSIC ROOMS

- Chairs
- Pianos
- Conductors' stands
- Music stands
- Instrument storage for wind, percussion, and strings
- Risers

CAFETERIA

- Tables with attached seating or tables with separate seating
- Seating for faculty/staff
- Sound system
- Kitchen with washer/dryer

MEDIA CENTER

- Lobby seating
- Student stations
    - Tables/chairs
    - Soft seating
    - Desks
    - Bookshelves
    - Computer laptop/Chromebook storage
    - Circulation desk
    - Sound system

SPECIALTY ROOM FURNITURE (IF APPLICABLE)

- Computer labs and chairs
- Manufacturing
- Project Lead the Way
- Work stools
- Health science
- Photography
- Art
- Agriculture
- Veterinary sciences
- TV production/broadcast journalism (equipment included under technology)
- Fashion design
- Culinary arts
- Drafting
- Engineering
- Architecture/construction

The specialty room list is based on potential secondary school offerings. Many specialty courses utilize technology and have been included with the computer labs. Many secondary schools offer courses with a school focus or theme and may include one or more of the courses identified. The furniture for those rooms is *content specific* and should be planned accordingly.

Other items to be included in the furniture requests are based on the building configuration and workspaces. The list may include such items as refrigerators, microwaves, and coffee makers.

Chapter 3

TECHNOLOGY

Technology is such an integral part of schools; it has been given its own chapter. Technology at one time was the use of devices for record keeping and student attendance. Over the past decade, technology is in every facet of the educational experience. It includes but is not limited to e-books in the media center, personalized learning devices, teacher devices, Promethean/SmartBoards, and online, standardized testing. Every classroom, as well as teachers and students, will have access to some form of technology every day. This chapter will include lists of items needed based on the category, and these categories are dependent on funding and allocations.

Most often, the technology budget is separate from the general allocations. If it is an opening for a new building and dependent on the school grade-level population plan, the technology budget is a multiple year allocation. The total dollars and the time frame for expenditures should be reviewed carefully. Additionally, the district "refresh" policies should be used when making the decisions in order to consistently maintain up to date and current access to technology for all stakeholders.

CLASSROOM

- Promethean or SmartBoard
    - Replacement bulbs
    - Docking station for computer access
    - Sound system

- Teacher/counselor/media specialist/administrator/police (SRO) devices
  - Laptops or desktops
- Office devices (include clerical, cafeteria, and maintenance)
  - Laptop or desktops
- Mobile Promethean or SmartBoards
  - Assess the need for mobile boards for specialty rooms and presentations in multiple locations and common areas in the buildings.
- Security system phones for building access
- Printers
  - The number of printers needed will be dependent on the building configuration, keeping in mind that all faculty and staff must have access to a printer.
- Copiers
  - The number and size of the copiers is dependent on the contract established within the school district or school sites.
- Student devices—personalized learning or shared devices
  - Laptops or Chromebooks

TVS

- Determine locations: cafeteria, media center, main office lobbies, common areas, and hallways
- Determine location for central programing.

PHONES

- Locations to be determined by the school site
- Individual offices: administrative, clerical, counselor, media specialist, and police
- Main office phone with student access available

- Conference rooms
  - Teacher access (individual or workroom access with assigned extensions)
  - Classrooms (phones or emergency button access)
  - Media center
  - Cafeteria
  - Maintenance

COMPUTER LABS

- Desktops with specialized program specifications and software
  - Engineering
  - Construction
  - Graphics
  - Drafting
  - Project Lead the Way (multiple components)
  - Architecture
  - TV Production

Specialized Program Equipment

TV PRODUCTION/BROADCAST JOURNALISM

- TV Cameras
- Handheld cameras
- Tripods
- Teleprompter
- Lan-C controller
- Studio intercom
- Video switcher
- Green screens
- Headphones

- Microphones
- Audio mixers
- Studio speakers

Chapter 4

ATHLETICS

Athletics has been a mainstay in secondary schools for decades, and the opportunities for interscholastic participation are even more expansive today for all students. There are many benefits to offering strong athletic programs in both the middle and senior high schools: teamwork, cooperation, social relationships, sportsmanship, comradery, commitment, leadership, time management, and purpose. Julie Foudy, former United States soccer player states, "Sports build good habits, confidence, and discipline. They make players into community leaders and teach them how to strive for a goal, handle mistakes, and cherish growth opportunities." (Edwards 2019).

With so many contributing factors, it is imperative to ensure that the facilities are not only aesthetically pleasing but also compliant with district and state competition guidelines (Chen 2018).

The different sports teams are dependent on the grade level and the district/state. For each sport offered at your school site, consideration must be given for the facilities, equipment, and uniforms. A list of the most common sports will be provided, and a checklist of items identified as necessary is included. This is by no means a complete list, but it should serve as a starting point. It is important to research each sport that is offered and create an exhaustive list of equipment that meets the safety requirements and needs of your programs. Most athletic program startup costs are a separate funding structure. It is important for initial purchases to fund as much equipment as possible. In my experience, once the athletic program startup funds are provided, there are no additional allocations for athletics. Continued funding for school

athletic programs is dependent on gate receipts, regardless of spectator participation.
- Football
- Volleyball
- Soccer
- Baseball
- Softball
- Wrestling
- Track and field
- Cross county
- Tennis
- Golf
- Lacrosse
- Bowling
- Swimming
- Badminton

SPORTS TEAMS

- Uniforms: home, away, and practice
- Equipment
    - Practice balls: racks and bags
    - Game balls: racks and bags
    - Nets: basketball, soccer, lacrosse, and tennis
    - Helmets: football, baseball, softball, lacrosse, and wrestling
    - Standards (soccer goal frames and volleyball poles)
    - Stands for the officials
    - Bases, soccer corner flags, and softball/baseball foul line flags
    - Field marking: spray machine/chalk
    - Scoreboard/controls
    - Rackets, bats, gloves, crosse, and clubs

Each sport has multiple options for game and practice equipment, and these options should be determined collaboratively with the school site athletic director and coaches as soon as possible. The determination for startup equipment will be based on available funding with an emphasis on purchases needed to address safety priorities.

Sports facilities are depicted in the architectural plans and built according to the architectural specifications. It is recommended that the specifications for the playing/practice fields/courts be reviewed in detail. A dimension that is even one inch too short creates a field that is not in compliance and could negatively impact a sport's record. In one school where I planned the opening, the plans called for two volleyball courts marked on the gym floor rather than one court in the center of the gym floor horizontal with the bleachers. If that had remained, the team would not have been able to play any home games because the court dimensions would have been out of compliance. In reviewing the gym and/or fields, please note the following for consideration:

- Gym markings for physical education classes and interscholastic sports
- Gym dimensions for physical education classes and interscholastic sports
- Gym placement of basketball goals, hanging lights, and sound systems/speakers
- Track markings for all events, including running, jumping, and throwing
- Football field: dimensions, markings, goal posts dimensions/placement, and sidelines
- Soccer: dimensions, markings, and goals
- Softball/baseball: dimensions for bases and pitching
    - In-play markers on the baselines
    - Safety fences and dugouts

School spirit and pride are essential components in building a successful school community. Athletic Programs are the catalyst for promoting a positive culture and a sense of belonging for students, staff, parents and community stakeholders.

Chapter 5

MEDIA CENTER

The differences between media centers ten years ago and today are staggering. The integration of technology has forever changed what a media center looks like and how it promotes research and the access to information. School media centers are an important hub of a school, and the traditional roles are quickly changing. Media centers need to adapt and redefine the spaces and purpose (Burleson, Fontinell, Lanier, and Nelson 2016). Students seeking information no longer need a physical space, so consideration must be given to different configurations in order to remain relevant. Not only must media centers create a comfortable learning environment but they must also expand opportunities for students to access information outside of the building (Krutz 2015).

In order to secure the core principles of a media center, decisions must be made that balance traditional and innovative goals. Traditional media center environments are geared toward helping students gather information. Media centers today are dynamic learning spaces, not just a place to warehouse books. The environment needs to be fluid and easily adaptable to the changing ways to access information and exchange ideas (Krutz 2015).

Students have become comfortable with multitasking, working in groups, and being surrounded by multimedia environments. Since students utilize many different learning styles, the media center should accommodate these trends with as many different learning spaces as possible: quiet study areas, group activity areas, spaces for individual and small group work, and areas for instructional presentations (Krutz 2015).

Physical considerations need to be carefully addressed with consideration given to how students will use the resources that are available.

Additionally, traffic flow patterns need to be analyzed to ensure that spaces such as the reading/study areas are away from high-traffic and noise-generating spaces (Krutz 2015).

As the school's information hub, the media center must be an environment that supports multiple learning activities, styles, and media formats. The amount of information available to students and teachers can be overwhelming. The media center staff help guide and teach students and other staff to cope with information overload and focus on what is meaningful and relevant to today's curriculum. A successful media center is a place where students can develop the skills and proficiencies necessary to succeed in lifelong learning (Krutz 2015).

Media center collections are part of the school accreditation process, and it is important to review the minimum requirements to ensure compliance. Allocations for collections are usually in a separate funding source, but decisions should be determined based on startup funding. Consideration should also be given to recurring funds, and a plan for multiple years should be applied to the initial media center setup. As discussed, collections must balance both hard copy and digital, depending on the technology and personalized learning opportunities for students.

COLLECTION GUIDELINES

- Age-appropriate materials
- Check the district list for acceptable reading titles.
- Orders are based on allocations.
- Digital and hard copies
- Mobile Promethean or SmartBoard for presentations

Furniture requirements are included in the chapter identifying furniture recommendations.

Chapter 6

ACCOUNTING

The allocations for startup funds are usually facilitated through the district office. Each district should establish a process for the expenditure of funds as well as a contact person for each separate budget, including but not limited to facilities, technology, media, athletics, and maintenance. Decisions regarding expenditures vary based on factors such as vendors and total cost. Expenditures over a certain amount require competitive bids, and the guidelines are typically quite specific. It is important to have district guidelines regarding the process with threshold amounts clearly delineated. Once the guidelines are identified and the allocations are provided, the purchases should be expedited as soon as possible (Cooper and Nisonoff, n.d.).

For new schools, the school site accounting procedures should be established approximately six months prior to the school opening or as soon as the treasurer/bookkeeper is employed. While accounts can be opened prior to having that person in place, it is much less complicated to have the treasurer/bookkeeper already in place due to the requirements for signatures and account access. The following are school accounting recommendations:

1. Identify a bank.
   - It is recommended to research the advantages and disadvantages of opening of a new school account (for instance, interest on money market accounts, penalties for returned checks, and access to statements). In today's markets, online banking guidelines should be considered, and you should ensure whether or not online banking is supported by the district accounting procedures.

2. Open a checking and savings account.
- School accounts require two signatures; one is the approver or administrator, and the other is the treasurer/bookkeeper. It is important to have a designee or backup for each of the two primary signers.
3. Obtain credit cards (P-Cards).
- These are generated through the district office and not directly with the selected banks. You will need credit cards for
  - School site purchases and
  - General fund purchases.

YEARBOOK AND SCHOOL PICTURE BIDS

Approximately three months prior to the opening of school, it is important to establish vendors for both school pictures and yearbooks. These are mentioned in the accounting chapter since both vendor selections are required to go through the competitive bid process. School districts have specific bid policies, and it is imperative that the guidelines are followed. Typically, vendor selections are determined with the input of a stakeholder committee: the school site administrator, teachers, parents, and students. Vendors submit a bid packet with detailed information regarding product offerings and cost analysis. After a review, the committee makes the selections based on the best features and cost. Typically, a one-year contract will be awarded the first year. After the school is operational and the school culture has been established, yearbook and picture company bids may become multiple year contracts as allowed by school district guidelines.

William Hartman defines education budgeting as a "working tool" for the successful operation of states and local school districts and as a "significant opportunity to plan the mission, improve their operations, and achieve their education objectives" (Hartman 1999).

Chapter 7

POLICIES AND PROCEDURES

School boards and district administrators have certain expectations about how a school should function and operate on a daily basis. In order to meet those goals, schools must establish clear policies and procedures. Policies and procedures are essential in defining expectations to ensure a well-managed, safe, and student-centered learning environment. They should also facilitate guidelines for stakeholder accountability. For new schools, creating policy is one of the most difficult and time-consuming aspects of establishing a school culture. The more comprehensive the school policies and procedures are, the easier it is to communicate them to stakeholders and apply them consistently to everyone.

A starting point for creating policy is to research the district-wide school site policies. All individual school policies must align with the district. I recommend a thorough review of school board policies and rules as well as the district handbooks. Any policy that addresses school site operations must be applied consistently. District policies are multitudinous and should be outlined meticulously. Policies should be organized based on various stakeholder groups. There will be policies that apply to students and parents, and there are other policies that apply only to teachers. There are policies that will likely apply to all groups.

Once the tedious process of outlining applicable district policies and procedures is completed, school-specific policies must be determined. It is always beneficial to review policy handbooks from comparable grade-level schools throughout one's district. It is helpful to see policies and review how the information is organized and presented to stakeholders. Since this is a time-consuming process, it is beneficial and expedient to utilize as much staff as possible. Once the information has been compiled with input from the planning team, decisions can be made and policies created to support the school's mission and vision and establish the school culture.

The following is a checklist of potential topics. It is impossible to list all the potential items, but this should serve as a generally accepted compilation of school site policies and procedures.

- Faculty sign in/sign out
- Daily schedule
- Student supervision and/or duties
- Hallway/passing supervision
- Supervision of after-school events
- Use of school equipment including but not limited to copiers, printers, faxes, phones, laminators, and poster makers
- Facilities guidelines: use of coffee makers, small refrigerators, heaters, fans, lights, and other small appliances
- Recycling
- Leaving during the school day
- Substitutes/class coverage: substitute lesson plans, seating charts, classroom procedures, and emergency contacts
- Personnel leave and absences: illness; parental, emergency, legal, and personal leave; bereavement; professional development; and Family Medical Leave Act (FMLA)
- Lesson plans
- Teacher websites
- Faculty grievances
- Faculty dress code
- Internal accounting: purchase orders, P-cards, travel, fundraising, and money collections
- Mandatory reporting: child abuse, sexual harassment, and bullying
- Safety: fire drills, emergency evacuation routes, lockdowns (full and partial), and severe weather

- Student attendance record keeping: daily attendance, classroom attendance, and tardies
- Early dismissals
- Grading
- Makeup work
- Homework
- Promotion/retention
- Building access specific to building configurations: doors, stairs, traffic patterns, courtyard access, common areas, cafeteria, gym, and auditorium
- Locks/lockers
- Announcements
- Hall passes
- Cafeteria procedures: breakfast and lunch
- Assemblies: topics, attendance, locations, and behavioral expectations
- Visitors in the building/classrooms
- Movies as classroom instruction
- Activity approvals
- Professional development funding requests
- Supplies/materials request procedures
- Fieldtrip procedures
- Guidance department services
- Student accidents/illnesses
- Emergency contact information
- Student information: Family Educational Rights and Privacy Act (FERPA), directory opt-out, media release, internet access, medical information, and special programs
- Electronic device policy
- Acceptable use
- Data security
- Certification guidelines: state/district
- Parent contact/conferences

- Code of student conduct/behavior plan
- Student dress code
- Bus, car, and walkers
- Identification badges

The more detail that is provided in a school's policies and procedures, the easier it is apply them consistently. School policies may be revised frequently to adapt to the changing dynamics of a school community. While a policy may work well one year, it may not work well in a different year. The key to successful policies is that they are fair, applied consistently, and assist in providing a safe learning environment. It is imperative to establish policies that can be enforced. Schools do not want to put themselves in a position of creating unenforceable policies. Doing so would immediately diminish the school leadership and control of school culture. School boards and districts revise and reverse policies, and schools must remain in compliance.

Chapter 8

HANDBOOKS

Handbooks are an essential component of any educational organization. They provide comprehensive information encompassing all aspects of daily operations. School boards and district administrators dictate district-wide policies that include federal, state, and legal compliance. School sites provide a more detailed, specific set of operational guidelines. School handbooks must provide relevant information to the stakeholder community for all levels of policy. Handbooks are created for the applicable groups and provide as much information as possible.

There may be times when stakeholders fail to follow the established guidelines. It is helpful to address concerns and provide a sense of accountability by providing stakeholders with a detailed handbook at the beginning of the year. The first page of any handbook should be a disclaimer page with a signature line. This form ensures that appropriate communication has been provided, and it outlines expectations regarding compliance.

All school sites are required to provide to stakeholders a faculty/staff handbook and a parent/student handbook. Any additional handbooks are at the discretion of the school site administrator. In line with the adage "more is better," it is recommended that other handbooks be on hand as well. A handbook for substitute teachers is critical. This handbook should include but not be limited to the daily schedule, bell schedules, record keeping, emergency contacts, and, most importantly, all safety procedures in the event of an emergency. Substitute teachers are invariably hard to secure, so a handbook goes a long way in helping them feel comfortable and safe.

Depending on the supervision configurations in your school district, you may want to include a separate handbook for custodial/maintenance personnel and noninstructional staff. The guidelines for these employees often include different policies for sign in, sign out, compensation, overtime, coverage, cross-training, and breaks.

Secondary schools should consider additional handbooks for athletics that include guidelines for coaches and ones for activities that include guidelines for club/class sponsors. Most coaches and sponsors are instructional staff regulated by faculty policies; however, there are instances where contract coaches and sponsors secure positions. It is prudent to offer a concise handbook with applicable information for their roles.

With the use of technology in the schools and the increase in school districts offering personalized learning, it is incumbent on the school to delineate the numerous guidelines regarding the use of devices. Personal device handbooks address rental fees, repair costs, acceptable use, and security.

The following is a recommended checklist of items to be included in the faculty/staff, parent/student, and substitute handbooks. It should be noted that there is redundancy with the list of potential topics for policies and procedures; however, as previously indicated, handbooks must include district-wide and overarching policies that would not be school specific. The organization of the handbook is at the discretion of the school sites. This checklist is in no particular order, but most of the district-wide topics are near the beginning.

FACULTY/STAFF HANDBOOK

- Opening greeting from principal
- Table of contents
- Personnel contacts
    - Responsibilities
    - Phone numbers and/or email contacts

- Quick reference guide for key contacts: administration, guidance, health services, main office, media center/technology coordinator
- Employment contracts/compensation guides
- Complaints and grievances
- Benefits guide
- Certification/qualifications
- Facilities' energy conservation protocols
- Professional leave: Family Medical Leave Act (FMLA), illness, personal, bereavement, military, professional, and vacation (twelve-month employees)
- Professional responsibilities
    - Code of ethics
    - Harassment/sexual harassment
    - Discrimination
    - Student/faculty/staff relationships
    - Separation of church and state
    - Political communication
    - Social media
    - Academic freedom
    - Copyright laws
    - Mandatory reporting of child abuse
    - Dress code
- Student publications
- Academic requirements
    - Uniform grading scale
    - Promotion/retention
    - Credit recovery
    - Graduation (high school)
    - Standardized testing
- Student Records: confidentiality
- Student information
    - Family Educational Rights and Privacy Act (FERPA)
    - Emergency contact

- Directory opt-out
- Internet access
- Media release
- Medical information
* Student behavior plan protocols
* Parent communication protocols
* Data security
* Acceptable use policy
* Tutoring for pay
* Student fees, fines, and charges
* Expectations overview
* Daily schedule
* Building access (specific to building configurations)
  - Doors
  - Stairs
  - Interior traffic patterns
  - Courtyard
  - Athletic fields/playgrounds
* Arrival/departure
* Student supervision areas/duties
* Supervision of after-school activities
* Location and use of school equipment
  - Copiers
  - Printers
  - Phones
  - Laminators
  - Poster makers
  - Report binders
  - Fax machines
  - Refrigerators
  - Coffee makers
  - Mobile Promethean/SmartBoards
* Leaving during the school day
* Class coverage: securing substitutes

- Substitute lesson plans, seating charts, and contact information
- Daily lesson plans
- Teacher websites
- Student record keeping
  - Homeroom attendance
  - Class attendance
  - Tardies
  - Grades
  - Individual education plans (for applicable students)
  - 504 plans (for applicable students)
- Academic requirements
  - Grading policy: tests, daily assignments, homework, and makeup work
  - Makeup work policy
  - Homework policy
- Early dismissals
- Hall passes
- Announcements
- Cafeteria
  - Prices
  - Procedures
  - Seating
  - Menu selections
- Assemblies
- Visitors in the building/classrooms
- Classroom movies
- Activity approvals
- Request for professional development funds
- Request for supplies/materials
- Request for maintenance
- Fieldtrips
- Fundraising
- Emergency assistance
- Student illness/accidents

- Media center
- Instructional materials: textbooks (hard copy or digital)
- Electronic devices (separate handbook recommended)
- Code of student conduct/behavior plan
  - Student expectations
  - Referral process
  - Parent contact
  - Consequences
  - Positive acknowledgments

PARENT/STUDENT HANDBOOKS

- Expectations
- Daily schedule: building access availability
- Bell schedules
- Identification badge (if applicable)
- Dress code
- Cafeteria
  - Procedures
  - Prices
- Student academic performance
  - Uniform grading policy
  - Makeup work
  - Homework
  - Report card/progress report dates
  - Promotion/retention
- Student attendance
  - Excused/unexcused absences
  - Absence notification/procedures
  - Tardy policy
  - Early dismissal
  - Perfect attendance requirements

- Student transportation
  - Bus procedures/behavior requirements
  - Car rider requirements/expectations
  - Walkers
- Health Services
  - Vaccinations
  - Medications
  - Chronic medical issues
  - Health room procedures
  - Illnesses
- Emergency procedures
  - Fire drills
  - Lockdowns (full or partial)
  - Severe weather
- Building access for parents/visitors
  - Volunteer guidelines
- Electronic devices (a separate device handbook is recommended for personalized learning schools)
  - Cellphone policy
  - Laptop/Chromebook policies
  - Acceptable use
  - Internet safety
- Code of student conduct/behavior plan
  - Expectations
  - Consequences
  - Positive acknowledgments

SUBSTITUTE HANDBOOK

- Sign in/sign out procedures
- Pickup
  - Daily schedule
  - Key

- Electronic device for attendance
    - Lesson plans
- Location of faculty/staff mailboxes
- School map
- Bell schedules
- Seating charts
- Security plan
- Location of emergency evacuation maps
- Location of phone/wall emergency buttons
- Location of faculty restrooms
- List of key personnel/contact numbers
    - Administrators
    - Department heads
    - Main office
    - Guidance
    - Health services
    - Custodians

The initial development of handbooks is both time-consuming and difficult. Determinations will need to be made regarding the topics to include and the order in which they appear in the handbook. If the handbook is to be used as a reference guide, it should include a table of contents and page numbers. Once the book is finished, it can be provided as a hard copy and/or digitally. Typically, handbooks are digital with one or two hard copies in common locations like the main office or media center. It should be completed after all the school policies and procedures have been finalized. School board and district policies can be taken verbatim from the district websites. All handbooks must be reviewed and revised annually.

Chapter 9

SAFETY

Families trust schools to be safe havens for their children. The unfortunate reality is that most school districts have already experienced or will experience some kind of crisis. Crises appear in many different forms, including natural disasters such as floods, hurricanes, tornados, and fires. It could also be a health issue such as a communicable disease or dealing with threats or school incidences of violence.

Due to recent violent events at schools across the country, there is a heightened level of urgency in placing school safety as a top priority. Nationally, school districts are updating buildings with security entrances, creating district-wide security plans, and providing intense trainings to deal with multiple crisis scenarios. Districts must rely on school staff to protect the children entrusted to them. School personnel must know what to do and how to accomplish emergency measures to help students in a crisis. Adults knowing what to do in a crisis can be the difference between life and death. The most important factor is preparedness (US Department of Education 2003).

The starting point for creating a school site crisis plan is to review the district crisis plan thoroughly. School districts have invested time, effort, and resources to update plans to address the escalation of incidences. School site plans must align with district plans to ensure continuity in the procedures. District procedures must be clearly outlined in the school site plan. Depending on available personnel, it is important to form a team to develop the plan. The team should include the principal, other administrators, noninstructional and instructional personnel, and other stakeholders deemed essential.

After forming the team and prior to the first meetings, make sure to have all the information needed to assist with the process. The district crisis plan must be available for reference. Additionally, as much information as possible should be known about the building. The architectural plans are most helpful.

The following plans/procedures must be developed for inclusion in the school site crisis plan. This is not a complete list, but it does cover most potential incidences.

- Evacuation maps
- Fire drill routes
- Lockdown drill: locations (may include relocations)
- Partial lockdown drill
- Tornado/hurricane drills (may include relocations)
- Access to entrances and security vestibule (if applicable)
- Exterior doors access
- Visitor sign in/scans and required identification
- Visitor access inside the building and/or badges
- Volunteer procedures
- Student ID badges (if applicable)
- Building key/badge access

Once the plans have been created with as much detail as possible, it is imperative that every person in the building knows his or her role. Plans should be developed for positions, not for specific individuals as personnel changes are not uncommon. Leadership roles are the most critical piece. While some responsibilities are automatically assumed, it is recommended that the roles fit the person's leadership ability. The suggested template below provides assistance in determining key roles. Always have a primary and an alternate in the event someone is not present at the moment an incident occurs. The template should include the actual names of the persons involved to leave no room for confusion.

School-Based Critical Incident Response Plan

SCHOOL-BASED TEAM

- Principal
- Assistant principal (AP)/designee
- Assistant principal: # in building
- Lead teacher/instructional coach
- School resource officer (SRO)
- School nurse
- Office manager
- Guidance
- Physical educator designee
- Psychologist
- Special education liaison
- Cafeteria manager
- Plant engineer/head custodian
- Teacher
- Parent

ROLES AND RESPONSIBILITIES

	Primary	Alternate
Critical incidence lead	Principal	AP/designee
School site communication		
Media liaison		
Campus security		
Classroom support		
Office services		
Counseling services		
Family support		
Medical/CPR		

Hospitality services
Memorial services/activities
Student accountability

    This form can be updated on a regular basis. Once the principal becomes more familiar with the faculty/staff, changes can made to ensure the most effective team leadership. This form should be concise and consist of only one page so that it can be used as a quick reference and kept in key locations such as the administrative and guidance offices, media center, and main office.

    Plans are useless if not communicated effectively to the affected stakeholders. The communication format is essential to the process and should be determined at the school site. Unfortunately, just having a well-communicated plan is not enough. Preparedness for incidences ensures that all stakeholders know exactly what to do and when to do it. Former United States Secretary of Education Margaret Spellings said, "Knowing how to respond quickly and efficiently in a crisis is critical to ensure the safety of our schools and students. The midst of a crisis is not the time to start figuring out who ought to do what. At that moment, everyone involved, from the top to the bottom, should know the drill and know each other" (US Department of Education 2003). The only way that happens is with practice. For example, most school districts require a minimum of ten fire drills a year. Since fire drills started, there are few incidences of students injured in fires. The drills provide the stakeholders the information needed to evacuate quickly and safely. The same should be true for all drills. They should be practiced frequently until everyone is comfortable with the process.

    Lastly, each school site should assemble and have available an emergency kit. It is important to include any equipment or materials that may be useful in any emergency. Typical items include a first aid kit, flashlight, blanket, megaphone, master school maps, a prepaid cell phone, and a radio.

    A safe learning environment is essential for students of all ages. Without it, students are unable to focus on learning the skills needed for a successful education and future. School safety is a twenty-four hours a day, seven days a week endeavor. Plans must be updated, monitored, and reviewed regularly for students to be safe in their school settings.

Chapter 10

SCHEDULES

Schools are tasked with providing students with learning experiences that will prepare them for all future endeavors. Every school must accept the tremendous responsibility of creating a curriculum that meets federal, state, and local guidelines while at the same time offering opportunities for students to excel academically and socially and acquire necessary skills for success.

Nationally, our vision for success in schools has evolved over time. Today, there are clear, rigorous standards designed to ensure students graduate ready for college and careers. Discussions regarding postsecondary experiences are now taking place in the elementary schools. Courses that once were offered only in high schools are trickling down to middle schools. There is increased accountability and a sense of urgency in helping students reach their goals.

The first part of this manual discusses the importance of creating a school mission and vision. The mission and vision are goals that a school curriculum must reflect. Whether it is a school theme or focus area such as Science, Technology, Engineering, Math (STEM) or Science, Technology, Engineering, Arts, Math (STEAM), International Baccalaureate (IB), Cambridge, Design and Architecture, Medical Services, or agricultural, the master schedule and course offerings must align and be reflective of those overarching common objectives.

The design, maintenance, and management of the master schedule are the total responsibility of the school principal. While parts of the process are delegated, the strategic thinking and decision-making is what drives the success of the school (Butterfoss 2018). Development of the master schedule starts earlier and earlier each year. The planning and building of the initial schedule should begin approximately ten months prior to the first day of school. There are many layers of building a master schedule, requiring a scaffolding approach that takes time and requires input from stakeholders.

Once a team is in place and the planning process begins, it is important to consider two of the most critical issues. The first is to have a basic idea of the projected student enrollment, which determines teacher allocations for the year. While it would be exciting to offer many elective courses in any grade level, the schedule must be supported by the number of teaching positions available. Additionally, depending on the restraints of the districts, it is important to adopt a bell schedule that meets the needs of the master schedule and course offerings. Some districts allow flexibility in creating a bell schedule while other districts have a uniform bell schedule for the grade-level configurations. Both allocations and bell schedules are discussed in more detail in other sections.

As with other chapters in the manual, the process of creating a master schedule will be outlined in a list format. Many of the items are used in all three grade levels while some are for only one grade level. The list can be used in full or in part depending on needs.

MASTER SCHEDULE PROCESS

1. Create an outline with completion/deadline dates for each part of the process.

2. Identify potential course offerings.

- Address school mission/vision and theme/focus.
- Address district initiatives.
- Address state/district requirements.
- Address instructional minutes.

3. List course offerings.

- Check viable state course code numbers.

4. Create a subject selection form for applicable grade levels.

5. Develop a comprehensive curriculum bulletin.

- Provide a brief description of each course offering.
- Include prerequisites and course requirements.
- Include projected fees (if applicable).

6. Determine number of projected positions/allocations.

7. Determine master schedule priorities (examples included below).

- Common planning period/time for departments
- Common planning period/time for grade levels
- Common planning period/time for teams
- Inclusion of co-teachers
- Inclusion periods/subjects
- Special education courses
- Teaming
- Common use of classrooms/facility

8. Develop a process for students to select courses (paper or digital).

- How is the process communicated and provided to assigned students?
- Include a statement that not all requests can be accommodated.
- Identify required courses.
- Elective options
- Remediation/acceleration options
- Parent review/approval

9. Enter the information into the scheduling system or master paper grid.

10. Once the course selections are entered, run a report indicating the number of requests for each course.

- Determine the number of total available classes/sections for core courses based on student ratios.
- Determine the number of total classes/sections for elective courses.
- Determine the number of classes/sections per subject/grade level.

11. Create a template for building a draft master schedule.

- Account for as many priorities as possible.
- Add the classes/sections.
- Based on certifications, add tentative teachers.
- Add room locations.

12. Build the schedule into the scheduling system.

- Schedule special education students first to ensure compliance with Individual Education Plan (IEP) guidelines.
- Schedule students into "singleton" classes (secondary schools).
- Schedule remaining students, accommodating as many student requests as possible.

13. Run a copy of the tentative schedule to make sure all components are included.

14. Run copies of individual student schedules to ensure:

- All required courses are included.

- Student requests are accommodated whenever possible.
- Students qualify for assigned classes by meeting federal, state, or district guidelines, IEP's, or other mandated programs
- Students have met course prerequisites and/or applicable assessments.

15. Provide copies of the individual schedules to students/parents for review.

Continue to refine the master schedule and adjust as needed to reflect changes in student enrollments, remediation requirements, and potential faculty changes.

BELL SCHEDULES

Many school districts across the country have a uniform bell schedule for specific grade-level schools. This chapter is geared more toward schools that have the flexibility to develop any bell schedule that meets the needs of the mission and vision as well as the theme and focus of the curriculum. There are many different options available to schools, including traditional schedules, block schedules, or a combination of both.

Schedules today must also take into consideration factors such as teaching models. Most recently, schools across the nation have incorporated project-based learning models. Project-based learning (PBL) is a teaching approach in which students, through projects, learn academic content, practice twenty-first-century skills such as collaboration, communication, and critical thinking and create high-quality, authentic products and presentations. In a PBL model, some educators recognize that time constraints hinder creative and innovative thinking, and extended periods may be beneficial (Liebtag and Ryerse 2017).

Another consideration must be given to state or local school district requirements for specific topics to be covered but not necessarily throughout the year. The schedules must accommodate these topics without negatively impacting the required instructional minutes for required courses. Examples of these topics are health education, sex education, character education, and student advisement times.

A starting point for the creation of your school's bell schedule is to research comparable grade-level schools in your district or in your neighboring district. This process will provide multiple examples of schedules and help identify the priorities based on course offerings and other requirements. As offered throughout this manual, the best way to provide the information needed to create a bell schedule is in a list format.

BELL SCHEDULE CONSIDERATIONS:

- Arrival/dismissal times
- Required instructional minutes for core courses
- Required instructional minutes for elective courses
- Required instructional minutes for selected topics
- Required minutes for lunch
- Required minutes for passing from one class to another
- Number of course offerings per semester/year
- Number of course offerings per day
- Type of teaching model: traditional or project-based learning

I recommend that several different bell schedules be drafted and reviewed. It is important, regardless of the flexibility of the district guidelines, that it be approved prior to the start of the year. It is also important to involve as many stakeholders as possible in finalizing the schedule. First and foremost, the schedule must be able to accommodate the school mission and vision while providing a safe and comfortable learning environment for all.

Chapter 11
INSTRUCTIONAL MATERIALS

Once the master schedule and course offerings have been finalized, the process of securing instructional materials for each course must begin. Districts have unique procedures for the selection of these materials based on state and local guidelines and allocations. As discussed in other chapters, the first step is to review the school site procedures and allocations. Some districts assume the responsibility of instructional material selections and ordering, and some districts allow schools the flexibility to complete the purchases at the school site. It is important to complete the selections and process as early as possible due to the time constraints of receiving the materials. The goal is to have all instructional materials in the classrooms before the first day of school.

While instructional materials include multiple types of resources, this chapter will focus on textbooks. Textbooks are a collection of the knowledge, concepts, and principles of a selected topic or course. Most textbooks are accompanied by teacher guides, which provide supplemental teaching materials, ideas, and activities to use throughout the academic year. Textbooks are still preferred resources because they are organized into units of work with detailed lessons and a chronological presentation of information. They also include teaching procedures and are based on the latest research and teaching strategies (TeacherVision 2019).

Instructional classroom materials come in two different forms. Hard copy textbooks are still available; however, many of these textbooks are available digitally. Schools with personalized learning devices use digital textbooks with a class set of hard copy books in the classroom. Either format requires every student access to the textbook material for each core course. Instructional materials for the core courses are based on the district's "adopted" books. These books have been selected by a district committee to ensure consistency within the district, grade level, and subject. Most textbook selections go through a district-wide adoption process and include supplemental/ancillary materials.

The Every Student Succeeds Act (ESSA) was implemented in 2015, requiring student accountability through standardized testing. Schools that have flexibility in ordering instructional materials must ensure that the text content aligns with the district standards. These materials must be beneficial in helping students achieve success on tested content.

Instructional materials are essential for academic success in all content areas. School districts, based on the ESSA requirements, prioritize funding allocations for core courses. It is equally as important to determine the allocations for elective courses and make decisions accordingly. Depending on the course and grade level, some textbooks for elective courses are required. High school courses for advanced placement, International Baccalaureate, and Cambridge require access to content-specific academic materials since they must complete and pass end of course assessments for credit.

Instructional materials are tools teachers use in the classroom, and they need these resources for success. The instructional materials designee in the school must work with the district liaison to ensure that all resources are available for the start of the school year.

Chapter 12

PERSONNEL/HIRING PROCESS AND LEADERSHIP POSITIONS

The success of any school is tied directly to the effectiveness of the faculty and staff. An important task is the coordination of a meeting with the head of the district's Human Resources (HR) Department to make sure their processes and procedures are followed in hiring. You will need the assistance of HR at every turn, so it is critical you work with them every step of the way. The goal of the district and the school site is to hire the most qualified and the best suited candidate for each position.

The hiring process should begin as early as possible, preferably five months prior to the first day of school. Teachers who apply for transfers to other schools must declare their intent early and offer schools the best selection of candidates. Transfer candidates are already vetted, understand the school district, and have accessible references. The meeting with HR staff will provide the specific hiring guidelines for both internal and external candidates. External candidates apply for positions as they become available and are a critical piece to filling all the open positions.

The next step is to identify your allocation positions and align the teaching positions with the tentative master schedule. The total number of open positions, the subjects needed, and the grade-level information are required prior to the first interview.

Listed below are key factors in the hiring process:
- Identify the number of open positions based on the district allocations.
- Work with HR to advertise the positions.
  - New schools may offer a faculty/staff meeting to provide an overview of the school, schedule, available positions, and expectations.
  - Indicate the minimum number of documents to be included in the application: resume, cover letter, and references.
- Form a committee that will screen and interview candidates.
  - Include administrators and available personnel in the same category of the open position.
  - Committee members may be different for various positions. It is recommended that the committee be consistent for the same position.
- Set a time and place for the committee to review and screen applications.
  - The number of candidates to be interviewed should be determined by the number of open positions in a single category/subject. The number recommended for an interview should be at least double the number needed. When screening candidates for interviews, ensure the candidate is eligible/qualified for the position. In most districts, anyone can apply to a position, so it is necessary to review all documentation carefully.
  - Instructional staff must be certified or eligible for certification prior to the state certification deadlines. These are the basic qualifications:
    1. Completed applicable coursework
    2. Passed all national, state, and/or local qualifying tests
    3. Holds a four-year degree (unless enrolled in an alternative certification program)

- Notify the candidates who are not selected for an interview.
  - Notification can be a call, letter, or email.
- Contact the recommended candidates and schedule them for an interview.
  - Determine if there is a one or two interview process for initial candidates.
  - Determine in advance the interview questions.
  - Complete a rating sheet (create one that meets your desired goals) to distinguish candidates from one another.
  - If it is a two-interview process, finalize a smaller number of candidates and complete the second interview with a different committee.
- Determine the recommended for hire candidates for all positions.
  - Notify HR of your recommendations.
    1. Internal candidates should be approved in the event there are no pending issues such as investigations, poor performance ratings, or they do not meet the minimum years in the same school.
    2. External candidates: HR completes the vetting process. Notify the candidates recommended for hire. Make sure they know the hire is not official until HR clears the candidate, and there are no guarantees for employment until they are cleared through the vetting process.
- Notify the candidates who were not recommended for hire.
  - Notification can be a call, letter, or email.

Before making the final decisions and offering a candidate a recommendation for employment, contact multiple references. Often, a candidate interviews exceptionally well, yet when the reference is contacted, the information is not favorable. Also, a candidate may not interview well, but the contacted references highly recommend him or her for a position. The interview process is a required and invaluable part of the process; however, the references are the most important component.

School personnel establish the school culture. Any person in the building who provides a service and/or interacts with students will have a lasting impact. The office staff is the first interaction students and parents have with a school, and positive impressions help create an atmosphere of inclusion. The custodial staff is critical to a safe and clean building, and the cafeteria staff provide meals for students (some who only have meals at school). Teacher-student relationships and the ability to help students find success are the end goals. Every position in the school must be filled with a qualified, dedicated, and caring individual, emphasizing the need to select only the best candidates.

LEADERSHIP POSITIONS

A critical piece of the hiring process prior to the start of the school year is to identify the leadership positions in your school. It is challenging for many reasons. One reason is because the new group has never worked together as a faculty and staff, and the group dynamics have not yet been solidified. Nonetheless, decisions on leadership positions need to be made to ensure a smooth school opening. Several positions in and of themselves are leadership positions: administrators, plant engineer/head custodian, and cafeteria manager. Leadership positions among the office and instructional staff are at the discretion of the school administration.

Depending on the district, a policy and procedure should be equitably established for identifying key roles. It is important that leadership decisions are made on an annual basis to allow for change as needed. For districts with teacher unions, guidelines for the selection of leadership positions are part of the contract negotiations and must be followed with fidelity, especially if leadership positions include monetary supplements.

Once the administrative team is in place, the responsibilities for each position must be clearly delineated and provided to the stakeholders. The document outlines the major areas of responsibility for each administrator and allows teachers a clear line of administrative support. Standard assigned responsibilities include but are not limited to grade levels, school safety, professional development, standardized testing, teacher observations, property/assets inventory, and activities/events.

Dependent on your grade-level configuration, leadership decisions should be based on multiple factors such as previous leadership experience, years teaching (minimal experience should be three years), interview responses, and interest in the leadership roles. Listed below are potential key positions. Many of the positions are for secondary schools only, but any leadership position should be based on the needs of your school.

- Grade-level chairpersons
- Department heads
- Learning community/team leaders
- Test chairperson
- Technology leader
- Activities/club sponsors
- Athletic coaches
- Yearbook sponsor

"Educational leaders play a pivotal role in affecting the climate, attitude, and reputation of their schools. They are the cornerstone on which learning communities' function and grow. With successful school leadership, schools become effective incubators of learning, places where students are not only educated but challenged, nurtured and encouraged" (University of San Diego 2019). This quote reflects the consequential impact of effective school leadership and the importance of making deliberate choices for leadership positons.

Chapter 13

BUSINESS PARTNERSHIPS

Educational institutions in all grade levels are charged with preparing students for postsecondary experiences and the world of work. Business leaders for years have complained that recent graduates are less prepared for the work force than students from prior decades. There has been a decrease in the ability of graduates to work independently and efficiently. In the past decades of rapidly changing technology and as schools continue to prepare students for work, school leaders have found the benefit of working directly with business leaders. Forming business and school partnerships is a productive way to bridge the gap between school and the world of work (Leatherwood 2007, 4).

Business partnerships include volunteerism, mentor support, workplace tours, internships, guest speaking, and other activities that facilitate the acquisition of skills such as creativity, innovation, critical thinking, and problem solving, collaboration and teamwork, communication, information, media, and technology. Additionally, opportunities to reinforce skills needed in the work force such as integrity, independence, self-motivation, work ethic, and interpersonal skills are encouraged (South Carolina Association of School Administrators 2017).

Typically, school districts have an established group of business partners. A starting point for a new school is to begin reaching out to businesses that already have a relationship with the district and have made a commitment to working with schools. Be selective in identifying partners initially to ensure a mutually agreed-upon list of support activities. It is not recommended that schools request funds as that is not the purpose of a business partnership. Depending on the working relationship and the nature of the business, monetary or equipment/material donations may be offered later.

There is no limit to the number of business partners that can be secured; however, it is better to work consistently with a smaller number than have little contact with a larger number. Below is a list of potential business partners. Contact initially the businesses that support your school mission, vision, theme, and/or school focus areas.

- Local chamber of commerce
- Hospitals and medical centers
- Grocery store chains
- Restaurants
- Local colleges and universities
- Engineering companies
- Construction companies
- Architectural companies
- Automobile manufactories/dealerships
- Banks, credit unions, or other financial institutions
- Attorney offices
- Law enforcement agencies
- Firefighters
- News media outlets
- Hotels
- Retail stores

Once the invitation has been extended and a business partner has agreed to work with the school, set up a meeting to discuss and define the partnership. It is important to outline how the relationship can be mutually beneficial. Create a proposal of potential activities, availability, and time constraints. If possible, work out a tentative schedule that can be referenced as the year progresses (Leatherwood 2007, 21). Lastly, select a contact person and school liaison. Businesses have limited time, and it is necessary to streamline all the requests through one person. This process will allow the business partners to prioritize activities and be assured the requests are approved in advance (Leatherwood 2007, 25).

Developing strong relationships with business partners is a critical piece of the education puzzle. Working collaboratively, school and business leaders can identify necessary skill sets and provide opportunities for students to achieve success and be better prepared for the world of work.

Dr. Herbert R. Fischer, former superintendent of San Bernardino County School, is quoted as saying, "So imagine if you will—education, business, industry, and labor align resources on behalf of lifelong student learning, resulting in a country-wide, business education partnership that has the potential to change the character of our region for the current generation and future generations to come" (Leatherwood 2007, 1).

Chapter 14

PARENTAL INVOLVEMENT

When discussing schools and educational opportunities, thoughts generally apply only to students. Parental involvement must be an integral part of the school equation because a child's success most often has a direct correlation to the level of the parents' participation. A parent's involvement—whether all in, all out, or somewhere in between—can be tied to a student's behavior, attendance, academic performance, and attitudes toward school. It is the responsibility of the schools to provide as many opportunities as possible for parents to become active participants in all aspects of his or her child's education (Silvertsen 2015).

When opening a new school, it is essential to include as many stakeholders as early as possible. As discussed in other chapters, stakeholder input is encouraged when making school-wide decisions such as school colors, mascots, and a variety of school policies and procedures, just to name a few examples.

There are several existing organizations that facilitate parental involvement. The best known is the Parent Teacher Association (PTA) or the Parent Teacher Student Association (PTSA). These organizations have national and state affiliations and stringent oversight. As required by those guidelines, these organizations must have a school site governing board and elected officers.

Based on my experience, I recommend that the initial parent meetings for a new school should take place approximately five months prior to the first day of school. By April, most school districts will have an identified school population plan and a list of potential students. It is recommended to research the surrounding feeder schools to identify possible parent leadership and make sure they are invited to the meetings. Also, work with the district parent liaison to help select an appropriate location and an effective method of communicating the meeting information to the applicable stakeholders.

While a school site PTA/PTSA has the discretion to determine the number of elected positions, all schools must have a president, treasurer, secretary, and parliamentarian. These officers should be the only positions elected initially. Once in place, they assume the responsibility for determining other officers and holding subsequent elections.

The first PTA/PTSA parent meeting is for the purpose of selecting a parent nominating committee as required. Since no officers are in place, generally an invitation is made to a local or state chapter to conduct the meeting. The purpose of the second meeting is to present the names of the parents recommended by the nominating committee and to conduct the vote. At the conclusion of the second meeting, the four PTA/PTSA officers will be in place.

Another avenue for parental involvement is the inclusion of parents on the school improvement council. Each school district may have a unique name for the committee, but it is a collective group of stakeholders who are elected and work together during the school year to address school issues and academic achievement. Generally, these committees do not have to be in place until after school begins. It is important to review the requirements for your school district and plan accordingly to elect school improvement council members.

Chapter 15

PROFESSIONAL DEVELOPMENT

Professional development (PD) in educational settings is defined as specialized training designed to help staff achieve school goals or intended to help educators improve his or her professional knowledge, skill, competence, and effectiveness.

For the purposes of this manual, PD will be the term used for training and/or meetings for all school employees prior to the first day of school. In a new school, no employee has worked together or has any knowledge of the school policies, procedures, or administrative expectations. The opening of school PD will need to be designed for specific groups, from clerical to custodial. The training must provide an overview and create a positive and comfortable environment prior to the arrival of students.

Professional development for the noninstructional staff will encompass training for their respective positions. For custodial and cafeteria staff, training is most often required at the time of hire and before they are assigned a school location. Professional development for these employees should be designed to familiarize them with the facility and with each other. It is especially important to create a sense of team and collegiality, and activities should be planned to accommodate those objectives.

It is recommended that the PD for the instructional staff take place approximately one month prior to the first workday. Based on the district hiring guidelines, the majority of the faculty should be hired by this point in time. There will always be exceptions and a few unfilled positions, but it is important to conduct the PD with enough time for the teachers to plan and apply the initiatives presented at the trainings.

The opening of school trainings is at the discretion of the school leadership. The main objective after the training is that the teachers meet the people they will be working with, understand the school's focus, and learn about the administrative expectations. Below is a sample agenda for an initial new school workshop.
- Introductions
- Mission
- Vision
- School goals/expectations
- School leadership expectations
- Team-building activities
- Group questions and share activity (both individual and whole group)
    - List positives that you hope to achieve as a school.
    - List positives that you hope to achieve as an individual teacher.
    - How can the administration help you achieve these goals?
- Teacher schedules and room numbers
- School tour (if possible)
- Secure supply wish list

The number of teacher workdays varies from district to district. Depending on the number of days available, it is helpful to include an opening of school workday schedule and agenda and provide it to the teachers. It assists them in planning and preparation and significantly reduces the stress for the unexpected. Workday meetings are generally outlined by the districts with specific topics that must be reviewed. This usually includes professional responsibilities, a code of ethics, and safety training. When opening a new school, everything is new, so it is important to allow for additional time to go over school site policies and procedures. Refer to the listings for both the policy topics and the faculty handbooks to drive the content to be discussed.

Chapter 16

COMMUNICATION

Communication is the process by which information is exchanged between individuals. In educational settings, effective communication with all stakeholders can mean the difference between a positive or negative reputation. School communities have an expectation that information will be free-flowing and current, and it is up to the schools to make sure those expectations are met.

Initial communication with the school community is challenging. Depending on the school opening date, the timelines for receiving potential student and parent information and timelines for building access meetings need to be carefully planned.

Students and parents are anxious to receive as much information as possible. Once the students have been assigned to the new school, a parent meeting should be scheduled. Plan for an initial parent meeting approximately three or months before school opens. This meeting is an opportunity for parents and students to meet the school leadership and receive an overview of the school's programs. The initial meeting should not be to discuss specific student schedules or school policies.

Most districts require schools to conduct parent meetings prior to the opening of school. These parent meetings usually fall within one week of the opening of school. If your district does not have this process but rather an open house after school begins, it is recommended that a parent meeting be conducted before school opens. Since there is no previous year on which to base school procedures, it is important to provide the parents and students the information in advance. This is also an opportunity to showcase and tour the new building, provided occupancy has been granted.

Students are invited to attend the parent meeting within the week before school begins; however, it is important that the first group to attend the new school be comfortable with the procedures and building. It is hard enough not to get lost in a familiar building, but it is extremely stressful for students of any age to struggle to find classes on the first day. Since parents and students receive information differently, it is recommended that the first meeting have two groups. Separate parents and students or conduct a separate student orientation at a different date and time.

The ways in which information is communicated to the stakeholder community has significantly changed over the past decade. School leadership needs to be deliberate in planning the most effective manner to disseminate information for your community (Andrade 2015). For instance, if your community does not have extensive access to the internet, social media may not be the best avenue. Also, be cognizant of language issues and provide translated papers if needed. It is helpful to start with the communication tools that will be consistently used. There is a comfort level when parents and students know where to go for information and in what format it will appear. Below are a few methods of providing information that have been used effectively.

- Social media
    - Facebook
    - Twitter
    - Instagram
- School website
- School Messenger (automated phone call system)
- Group email
- Newsletters (mailed)
- Google classrooms
- School announcements
- School media announcements on TVs

With all the communication tools that are available, schools have little excuse not to remain current and keep an open line for all stakeholders. While stakeholders may not always agree with the information, they tend to respect that it was provided to them in a timely manner, and it allows them to plan accordingly.

EPILOGUE

In July of 2013, I retired from the Miami-Dade County Public School System, the fourth largest school district in the nation. I am still in awe of the educational experiences and opportunities that I witnessed and was a part of for almost thirty years. But, having grown up in South Carolina, I knew it was time to go home. It just so happened that my hometown of Greenville, SC, had recently advertised a principal vacancy to open a new middle school.

It is hard to explain, but I was not quite ready to leave education all together. When exploring my options, I decided to apply to the Greenville County School District for the principal position at the new school. Fortunately, I was offered the job, and I and accepted the challenge.

I was part of two school openings in Miami, so I was confident that I was up to the task. The first step I took was to research any materials that were available to assist with the process. I was certain that the resources would be unlimited. I was wrong. I was unable to locate a manual that addresses how to open a new public school from the time school leadership is assigned until the first day of school. I am not suggesting there were no available resources, but I was looking for a concise manual that included lists of to-do items. I wanted but could not find a manual from which I could pick and choose what I found to be beneficial.

In July 2018, I actually retired again—this time for good. With that said, I had enough time to write the manual that I so desired as I planned a new school opening. School districts in all corners of the world at some point or another open a new school. It is a long, tedious endeavor, and if this manual can offer any assistance, it will be one of the most rewarding experiences in my life dedicated to education.

ACKNOWLEDGMENTS

I want to thank all of the school district leaders who were willing to take a chance on me. I am grateful for those who saw in me the potential to be a school site administrator.

Thank you to the thousands of students I have worked with over the years. You have shown me why I am a lifelong educator and why the sky is the limit for our youth.

Thank you to the hundreds of faculty and staff I have worked with. We worked together to create opportunities for students and to prepare them for life in the real world.

Thank you to the many faculty and staff that have become family. My life is enriched because of those nurtured and lifelong relationships.

Thank you, Dr. Margaret Haun, Laurie Schmotzer, and Kim Skipper for your valuable input and assistance.

REFERENCES

Andrade, David. 2015. "The Importance of Communication in Education." *Tech & Learning.* https://www.techlearning.com/tl-advisor-blog/8716.

Burleson, Todd, Diane Fontinell, Jennifer Lanier, and Katie Nelson. 2016. "Rethinking the
Library Media Center." *K-12 Blueprint.* https://www.k12blueprint.com/success-stories/rethinking-library-media-center.

Butterfoss, Jennifer. 2018. "7 Steps Principals Can Take to Deliver on an Awesome Master Schedule." *School Leaders Now.* https://school-leadersnow.weareteachers.com/school-master-schedule/.

Chen, Grace. 2018. "10 Reasons Why High School Sports Benefit Students." *Public School Review.* https://publicschoolsreview.com/blog/10-reasons-why-high-school-sports-benefit-students.

Cooper, Bruce S. and Phillip H. Nisonoff. (n.d.) "Accounting Public School Budgeting and Auditing: Budgeting, Accounting, Auditing, Future Trends." *State University.com.* https://education.stateuniversity.com/pages/2342/Public-School-Budgeting-Accounting-Auditing.html.

Edwards, Alex. 2019. The Clarion. *Swimming for a Purpose.* https://connersvilleclarion.com/1001/sports/swimming-for-a-purpose

Gabriel, John G. and Paul C. Farmer. 2009. *How to Help Your School Thrive Without Breaking the Bank*. Alexandria: Association for Supervision and Curriculum Development. E-book.

Hartman, William T. 1999. *School District Budgeting*. Reston: Association of School Business Officials International.

Krutz, David. 2015. "Libraries Media Centers." *School Planning & Management*. https://www.webspm.com/Articles/2015/06/01/Libraries-Media-Center.aspx.

Leatherwood, Jim. 2007. *Facing the Future Together: Forming Successful School-Business Partnerships*. Riverside: The Brooke Press.

Liebtag, Emily and Mary Ryerse. 2017. "Scheduling for Learning, Not Convenience." *Getting Smart.com*. https://www.gettingsmart.com/2017/02/scheduling-for-learning-not-convenience.

South Carolina Association of School Administrators Roundtable, Greenville County Schools. 2018. *Building A Better Graduate*. http://www.greenville.k12.sc.us/Parents/docs/gradplus_brochure1611.pdf https://www.greenville.k12.sc.us/Parents/docs/gradplus_brochure1611.pdf

Silvertsen, Juliette. 2015. "The Importance of Parental Involvement in Your Child's Education." *Washington Christian.org*. https://www.washingtonchristian.org/blog/the-importance-of-parental-involvement-in-your-childs-education.

TeacherVision. 2019. "Textbooks: Advantages and Disadvantages." https://www.teachervision.com/curriculum-planning/textbooks advantages-disadvantages.

University of San Diego. 2019. "The Secrets to Successful School Leadership." *University of San Diego.* https://onlinedegrees.sandiego.edu/the-secrets-to-successful-school-leadership/.

US Department of Education. 2003. "Practical Information on Crisis Planning: A Guide for Schools and Communities." https://www2.ed.gov/admins/lead/safety/emergencyplan/crisisplanning.pdf.

The School District of Greenville County does not endorse this book or the contents contained herein.

www.ingramcontent.com/pod-product-compliance
Lightning Source LLC
LaVergne TN
LVHW011855060526
838200LV00054B/4343